LET'S FLIP THIS DIAMOND HOUSE

THE ESSENTIAL GUIDE

TO HOUSE FLIPPING

SECRETS TO SUCCUSES IN
ANY REAL ESTATE MARKET

CONTENTS

Chapter 1 - Why A Diamond ?

Chapter 2- Gathering Knowledge and Using your Natural Wisdom

Chapter 3 - Do your Research

Chapter 4 - Contractor estimates, proposals invoices and payments

Chapter 5 - Buying, Making or Breaking your Dreams.

Chapter 6 - Let's Flip This Diamond !

Chapter 7- Keeping motivation while flipping houses

Chapter 8-In the Chapter we will review the going rates for different remodels in 2024.

CHAPTER ONE
WHY A DIAMOND?

CONGRATULATIONS ON YOUR NEW ADVENTURE INTO THE AMAZING, HUGE HOUSE FLIPPING INDUSTRY. I HOPE YOU WILL HAVE ALL THE SUCCESS YOU DREAM OF, AND I HOPE THAT EVERY IDEA YOU HAVE WILL MANIFEST ITSELF INTO THE BEAUTY AND AMAZING RENOVATIONS YOU WILL MAKE FROM THIS POINT ON. I WISH YOU HAPPY FLIPPING DAYS AND SUPER
SUPER PROFITABLE DEALS!
READ ON TO LEARN SOME GREAT TIPS AND SECRETS ON HOW TO SUCCEED IN THIS MARKET AND MAKE A LIVING BASED ON ASSETS AND SECURE INVESTING!

Today you have made the decision to open this book and read about how to flip a Diamond House. Every house can become a diamond house if you put your effort into it and make it special for the new buyers. Remember you have the tools in your hands to make this shine and strong. You're the carpenter even if you are not the contractor.

You are the Artist of your canvas, you will contribute to this house your emotions, your ideas and your time. You must look at it as if it is your Diamond in the Rough, that you have dug up and found to be made new and whole.

    Well let's just say not literally a Diamond house but maybe something like one after its true colors are revealed. You have made the decision to find a goal accomplished. You have been working and pondering this great idea of purchasing this property whether your first or not and making magic happen.
    Why a Diamond house you may be asking, well because every house You find and dedicate yourself to, every house that you make shine and light up, polish, give off its brilliance on that street and is awakened should be considered a Diamond. Because of the lasting life you will give it Remember Diamonds are forever!

    This is not your ordinary House flipping Book This book will give you reliable information, true situations that you may be faced with and awesome first-hand advice on how to achieve what you have sought out to do.

I have included several tools in each Chapter to help in your House Flipping process, as well as real pictures of one of my Diamond flip houses. There are certain questions that you should always ask yourself in your evaluation process when getting ready to purchase a house and I have included those tips and tools as well.

Now by all means I do not have all the answers and you may not even agree with some of my advice, but if you can carry away with you even 1 thing learned to help you accomplish you goal then I am thrilled and reading this book has definably been worth the complete effort.

In this treasure hunting career path or hobby of flipping houses we all need to continuously strive to learn new tips and be pushed to keep going. I believe completely in seeing is believing and tools to help us, we as humans can accomplish anything.

This information will give you more knowledge of the bumps and obstacles that are also involved with house flipping. My goal is to be able to share the truth about house flipping with as many people as possible so that way, everyone that is ready to flip their Diamond house will be able to do so with confidence and power to fulfill their dreams.

All our goals can be accomplished merely through thinking it can be and pushing through the path to get there. We must put into our minds at the beginning of any task whether small or big that we will succeed and make this the best darn thing we can do, and our mind's energy will begin to put the belief into place for us.

If even better we look at the project as already done and just needing to make the steps to get to the end to where it already is then it will make our goal seem more effortless, more rewarding and hobby oriented instead of just a task that needs to be fulfilled.

We as humans must learn first, gather knowledge and wisdom and then put into these into action to be able to excel at are Dreams and Goals. That's Right those will be your First steps to house flipping even before you find the house.

Stop and take a deep breath, relax and say to yourself [The knowledge I will gather will completely steer me in the most positive direction] .

Then not only will this knowledge steer you into the most positive direction but also it will steer you directly into your first house to flip and ever one thereafter .The homes that are made to our amount of knowledge will begin to feel almost as though a magnet is pulling you closer before you know it every home that you flip will begin to have somewhat of the same qualities as the previous and the one before that .

Also, we will gravitate at times to homes that remind us of a pleasant moment in our lives, a memory perhaps that brings on a good feeling or vibe for you. And then Bam out of the blue, you will start to pick your homes or as I say they will start to pick you!

This book will really be a type of short, but sweet book .One of those easier to read type packed with a lot of info in a small amount of time type of books .Those are the type that allow us to skim through with little effort pull out what we need for ourselves ,compare with others opinions and then put to work and use right away without wasting any of our valuable time .

As you will quickly realize as an investor Time is so valuable, and Time literally is money!

After you have gathered your knowledge, you are at the next position, once again relax and allow now your natural Wisdom to take over and be your guide for the next month to 2 ,3 ,4 months of your project and your Diamond House.

Knowledge and Wisdom are such important key factors in this Business or hobby that you are pursuing. It is not just intelligence or physical strength to build and fix things. It is these important gifts that will help in this and in every aspect of your life that will truly make things run smoothly and with such ease and awesome energetic vibration.

By using these gifts or tools you will make things just start to fall into place all around you. You will bring all the right people around you to actively help you with your project, you will deter all problems and handle obstacles with ease and grace. This will be given to you by First the knowledge that you gathered prior to starting and then by your natural Wisdom.

Wisdom will respond to your complete comfort level positively because of your comfort, due to the amount of knowledge you have assumed prior to starting. We will discuss gathering knowledge in the next chapter and how to awaken your Natural Wisdom inside. These are the crucial first step to locating the right house and getting it for the right price.

One of the most important things to remember when flipping a house is to always flip it correctly and properly. Chapter 5 in this book will provide you with information on flipping house properly and these can ultimately make or break your house flipping dreams.

What we need to remember is things done correctly will always be rewarded in due time.

- We will look at profits, and how to maximize profit. Not little profit that people speak about for a side part time Job or that you see on TV shows. Where you see all this hard work and sweat, and mistakes turn into 5 to 10k at the end of the flip. If you are putting in all the time and effort to thinking about your dream and then all the time and effort putting your dream into action, then you must make sure you will be rewarded. You should have enough funds to outlast your stress from the month or two that were just put in.

In this book that you will be reading about how earn larger profits from house flipping, not to settle for a month or two of paid bills but accomplish a 20 to 30k profit every time. You will learn a lot of pointers and tips. Later in Chapter 3 we will start to look at difference in spending and how to maximize profit.

I have put together real numbers used to buy and sell my properties, straight true numbers so that way they can be used for your comparison purposes when looking at properties. Now not all states and cities property values are similar but by familiarizing yourself with the estimated numbers I have provided. These will once again help you gain more knowledge of negotiation and the house flipping process. These numbers of facts, proposals, estimates and situations can be used for getting the most out of every flip.

We will discuss Contractor estimates, proposals invoices and payments in Chapter 4. By the time you read this Chapter it will be like turning on a light in a dark room. Normally it is so hard to get real numbers to look at, but I will share some of mine with you in this book to use as tools.

I am ready to dive in and start showing you the ins and outs of Flipping this Diamond house.

So, if you read this book from start to finish you will surely be on the path to success in your house flipping goal, Let's Make some money !

Chapter 2
Gathering Knowledge and Using your Natural Wisdom

Wow, I have to say these will be your most important steps to making the house flipping process to go as smoothly and full of force as possible.

First let's look a little at These two Gifts:

Knowledge: in the dictionary is explained as an acquaintance with facts or principles.
So, since we know that this is what Knowledge consists of then we automatically see how incredibly important it is to achieve our goals of House flipping
Wisdom: The quality of being Wise, Knowledge of what is true and right combined with just Judgment.

The 2 go hand in hand, so with one can be acquired the other.

Knowledge is a very important quality to have Knowledge is used in Everyday living and helps us completely go through are day. There are different characteristics of knowledge that help us accomplish different things in life. As we make go through each day, we are using different types of knowledge to be able to correctly take actions in this world. What we use frequently are Basic Knowledge and Learned or acquired knowledge.

Basic Knowledge includes all the basic things we know and have learned to be able to function properly. Knowledge to stop at a red light, or to tie are shoes before walking or the knowledge to get up at a certain time for work. We use the basic functions on a day-to-day basis and have become accustomed to these, so they have been formed and excessed properly. In some parts of the world these would not be considered basic knowledge since these are not ever taught or used.

Then we have are learned or acquired knowledge which is what really set us apart from everyone around us and makes each person an individual. This one is what we decide to use, when we want to use it or are told to use it.

This type of knowledge is truly the awesome knowledge to have because based on the amount of knowledge to we acquire or learn is the amount of intelligence we must be able to acquire Wisdom and what we want in life. Our life's goals and dreams begin to form and be put into action with this type of knowledge.

We are taught in schools and from books and reading and with experience and hands on project about a certain subject or idea .We begin to gather information about that idea and know this idea or subject has officially became knowledge in our minds ,it has officially found a space that has been filled inside of our minds and been implanted there for a period of time .Know depending on how interesting this idea or subject is to us is how long it actually stays our learned knowledge.

For example, when I was a child I had a rough childhood, my parents were very poor they had come to the United States in the 1980s from Europe seeking a better life and freedom from communism. At this time, they did not know the language and had no choice but to learn it to be able to live here and fit in to society.

I also had to learn and learning was never my favorite thing in school I had a very hard time and would actually walk out of my classes if I did not understand something or was not interested so in those subjects I did not acquire knowledge. Algebra and math were always my least favorite subjects, so I never wanted to learn those subjects.

So, this shows us that if the idea or subject is not important to us to our very selves, to our mind and they bore us or us not from our true desires or talents they will not become us or shape us they will not become a knowledge that we keep for a long time. It will either become temporary knowledge or will never even be learned.

What we need to focus on in life is finding knowledge all the way back from childhood that becomes who we are today and helps shape us into prosperous healthy individuals.

We must acquire knowledge that is able to be used to achieve our goals and become are identities. When I began buying and flipping houses, I had this passion for it, this push that said, "do this because you want to learn about it and feel it."

    There was this excitement that stirred inside of me, and I began to want to know everything about the process of flipping houses. I began to research day and night about how to start. I began to gather knowledge about flipping house from every place I could, watching shows, reading books, driving neighborhoods that were being flipped. It was knowledge I wanted to acquire, and it began to shape me. The passion had been awakened and was there, there was no stopping me.

    This type of knowledge is the best it becomes easy to acquire because we are interested in acquiring it. Not everyone can flip houses or maybe they will flip and then they do not continue because this is not their passion.

    If it is something that is not inside of ourselves truly and if we don't have a passion for it will be hard to learn the knowledge accurately and then it will be hard to shape us to follow that idea or subject. I this point is when it becomes just that an idea and subject rather than a dream or goals.

Any type of knowledge learned that has benefited us or helped us learn something that we did not previously know and made us wiser becomes Wisdom. Wisdom is a gift that needs to be taken very seriously and needs to be listened to reproduce more of it and keep that gift strong. It is a never-ending gift with unlimited potential and needs to be respected and put to benefit us and others around us. Listen to it ,It is trying to help you it will guide you in all your major life paths !

Wisdom when used correctly will help thousands of people we meet or interact with and will heal, support, guide and purify. Wisdom will only be given to those who seek it with honest earnest hearts. This will be discussed more in Chapter 6 make or break your goals.

So, when we find our passion to flip houses this will always be first step gather knowledge. We must know that the process takes time and will have different obstacles to overcome so if we do our research ahead of time it will ultimately be what gets us doing exactly what we are dreaming of doing.

Chapter 3
Do your Research

Research is essential to being able to locate the correct property you are looking for. Flipping houses is commonly mistaken as something that can be done quickly and with minimal funds. This information is incorrect and cannot be trusted. With anything that is done quickly and for very little so will be the outcome.

In this chapter you will learn important information before buying a flip house This list that I have put together for you should be used a reference to look at when actively getting ready to purchase the home it will help you determine if this home is a Diamond or a Dud.

If you can gather the information to answer these questions then after you have the answer, you can look at the facts and Knowledge about that house that have been exposed due to the research done. Never buy a flip house in a hurry, if the house goes under contract before you get a chance to look at it or if another contract gets accepted it is because you were not meant to have that specific house.

    Houses have different issues, difficulty level and energies in and around them and this is very important to consider before jumping into any large project. The right home will so to say, "speak to you" and when it does everything you do to that home will go exactly as it was supposed to go.

    There have been times I have seen two or three buyers fighting desperately for one home going back and forth bidding higher and higher until one of them gets it and they either got it for too much now and they cannot make the profit they had originally estimated, or they got the wrong home, and the homes energy was not meant to be theirs.

    They will fix it differently then they previously wanted to because of the fact they had to bid higher to get it and that took away from fixing costs. And then when they go to list the house it sits longer than anticipated on the market because it was missing that special amount that could've be included if not for the bidding war at the beginning.

Remember the energy you bring into a home is the energy that will surround you and that home throughout the whole process .So in the case mentioned above the buyers energy changed due to the fact that they had to pay more for the house and then they had to take out of what they had planned to do ,so that added confusion and anxiety upfront to their project.

This is where we must take what we learned in Chapter 2 about knowledge and Wisdom and apply it. When researching for a property there are common factors to consider and those are called

Buy Factors - Sell Factors
Let's take a look at Buy factors they include a variety of things we need to consider when getting ready to buy our flip house.

BUY FACTORS

1. What is the asking price?
2. How long has the house been on the market ?
3. What is the potential for resale?
4. Will my investment be safe?
5. Will I have sufficient amount of funds to cover the remodel?
6. What is the school district?
7. What are my comparable?
8. What is the inventory for sale like in this area?
9. Where are the nearest highways located?
10. Where are the local Police Departments, Fire Departments, Post Offices Located in distance to this potential property?
11. What are the property taxes ?
12. Are there any back taxes or liens on the property?
13. Who were the previous owners and what happened to make them sell?
14. Is this a foreclosure?
15. Will this house need extensive work or as they call it in the Real Estate industry Lipstick repairs?
16. If the house needs extensive repairs what will this mean to you?

SELL FACTORS

1. Can I sell this house and make a reasonable amount of a profit?

2. Will this home sell quickly due to the area?

3. Will this home be able to accommodate enough people or a family?

4. Is there more than 1 bath in the home?

5. Will the Buyers be happy enough with the house to be able to take on the mortgage payment especially if it is on the higher side?

6. Will the buyers be happy with the improvements made to the home?

Huge Tip #1 Do not go and search for a property looking for the lower price. Lower priced properties are not always your best option.

There's lots of circumstances that must depend on that property is a very key factor in where the property is situated the neighborhood is a very big factor school district. A lot of times families relocating are trying to get into a specific school district for one reason or another, so possibly buying closer or walking distance will always help in the long-term portion when you list you home .is a very big factor.

The type of work you're going to have to put into it as well as the environment around it A lot of times the lower priced properties have a great extent of work that needs to be done to get it back to shape and then if you want to take it above and beyond that will up the investment you are putting into it. Older homes to require a lot of time and money to be invested and usually will pull up some hidden surprises when it comes to out-of-pocket expenses.

Step 2. Looking for a property if you are thinking Hmm, I want to make this a quick flip and from the outside might look like it at first. To make this a quick flip you need to look at all the aspects of the properties job before you can say this is going to be a quick one. This goes back to the second chapter about gathering knowledge, we definably need to do this when we have located a property that might suit our interest and accommodates our price range. Do your research here find out all background on the property, flood zones, basement repairs, sewer lines etc...

    These houses are sometimes the ones that end up surprising us with that hidden broken septic system or a great big underground pool that was filled in and never maintained.

    Interesting situation about people that go out and buy properties that are thinking I'm going to buy this house and I'm going to put roughly $20,000 into it. Quick flippers don't realize is that you must look at the aspects underneath you have to take the veil off you take the curtain down, Behind the Walls. You don't want to fall into that problem at the very end of your project when the inspector comes in. This is worst case scenario for everybody.

    Lots of opportunities are available in flipping houses but sometimes the best opportunity is not getting the cheaper priced house. Trying to put roughly $10 ,000 to $20,000 into it and saying done and listing it. Where did the passion go when this happens?

Where did that initial energy go if you sell like this and only make about 5 to $10,000 profit for 3 months of works is it worth it then? Those kind of houses are part time houses if you are looking to only spend about one to two months in it and you made yourself probably anywhere from an extra $2,500 an extra $5,000 in that month nice yes., but if you end of spending more time fixing it 3 months then your profit starts to decrease and what about the time it sits on the market ? All these needs to be taking into consideration and are all circumstances that happen.

Chapter 4
Contractor estimates, proposals invoices and payments

So, what's next well let's review a couple things we have gone over, the property must be located and that takes a good time 30 days roughly to find the property, do the inspections necessary. All the inspections gone cheap on this part of the project will never benefit you. There are so many important things to be inspected in a property. Here is a list of some of the biggest expenses we will look at that almost always come up when flipping a property.

1. The Roof -defiantly one of the biggest and most common repairs you will have. Words of advice and wisdom get yourself a great Roofer that will be reliable and one that can say I don't subcontract my Jobs. Getting a Roofing company that does not subcontract their jobs to other crews will save you thousands of dollars on a Roof. Also, usually you can save even more if the owner if the salesman and instead of just a salesman. These 2 things have saved me anywhere from 3K on a smaller Roof Job to 8 k on a large one it makes a huge difference.

2. The Foundation -big problems happen here always have a professional look and inspect the foundation for any cracks, shifting, bowing caving or sinking going on here. As we all know the foundation of every house is the beginning and that whole house sits silently on that foundation so any problems, there will be very important to address. Foundation repairs are not cheap repairs and the minimum I have spent ever on a foundation repair was 2k and that was just for some cracks. The foundation of everything is so important it is the beginning of successes let's pay extra attention to it then.

3. The Electrical- this is by far in the list of top expenses. This one is always my pet peeve for sure. See these electrical companies vary so much on their pricing its almost hard to trust which one is being honest. This pricing is so ridiculously up and down it is almost unbelievable. So, I think the same thing goes here as well. As mentioned for Roofing get yourself a wonderful electrician that is trustworthy licensed and insured, you will need to.

This is one of those 2 peas in a pod type of relationship. I always double check on my reliable contractors, and they know that and try to stay fair and honest. I was once given 3 completely different electrical bids on the same job performing the same work with the same exact materials it was outrageous. I had collected the first bid for 11,750 the second for $9500 and the final one I went with was $6,300 and it was from a more popular electric company too. Imagine my relief I got to do all kinds of little extras everywhere with that savings. **Huge Tip #2 Always gather more than 1 estimate in the first portion of your house flipping Until you know the pricing yourself you never know who could be trying to pocket a couple extra bucks.**

4.The Plumbing -This is another huge repair that you will need to always take into consideration. Older houses almost always require new plumbing pipes put in and a lot of the time a whole house of new plumbing is mandatory when you get an inspector.

Typically, the newer side of houses will need at least basic plumbing updates such as a new water heater, new fixtures, new garbage disposal, updated dishwasher pipes etc. If you are doing new plumbing throughout the entire home, you can add some cool updates to the plumbing such as a tankless water heater which might catch a buyer's eye. Then there is the debate on piping which there is always the new way to go which is called Pec, but I like to stick with the good old copper piping and for just a little bit more you can still get a certified plumber to install that for you. Plumbing is usually easy to get accurate bids on so yes get more than one bid, but this is one that will not vary to much from plumber to plumber. The things to look out for with your plumbing or plumbing inspections that can bring in extra costs quickly would be a septic system or well. Septic systems in older homes are almost always not functioning properly because of the older materials that they were using when first installed or because of not doing proper regular maintenance or excessive use.

Depending on the area different types of septic systems can be installed .Also there is always the option of connecting to public water supplies where perhaps there wasn't before .If you have the option of connecting to public water and sewer services it is a great idea to take this option and not think twice about it .I have seen septic repair get extremely costly and depending on the system or full replacement can run as high as the $20,000.

5. The Well- this is a neat expenses and utility if you run into it. There are options on this. First if you have the option to keep it and just hire a well contractor to replace piping and get it working great. If the whole well system needs to be replaced it can get costly so once again if public water is available hook up. Any Well that is not in use needs to be properly capped off with cement and sealed properly, all the codes on sealing a Well properly in your area should be checked with your local building code and enforcement office. At times Wells can be hazardous so always pay attention and act on the side of caution when you have discovered one.

Some Wells may also be considered Historic and this case they will be listed in a Historic register for Wells. So definably dot all your I; s and cross all your T's on this one.

Other Contractors that will be valuable to have on speed dial would be a good

6. Drywall crew, this price can vary tremendously so if you can find referrals on this one that is a good route to go. If you do not have a referral that can be given you can always try calling a local apartment complex and ask the office staff for the company's phone numbers that they use as well as their painters. This is a bit of a secret but if you are very polite about it, they will hand that info right over maybe they will even throw in their.

7. Carpet flooring contractors. This is called cut the middleman out and get straight to the source of the pricing. These contractors usually charge rock bottom pricing to the apartments because of the flow of quantity they give them. Just make sure to mention who referred them and they won't try to cover charge since they have to stay comparable to the other pricing, they are giving out.

8.Then you have. foundation repair specialists which are good to find nearby and one that can come out quickly and do minimal repairs. Let's not try and open any foundation worms if we don't half to. Just always make sure you have the experts in on this one so they can provide you with warranties. Make sure your foundation/basement is always waterproofed and has no leaks. Any bowing of cracking from the bottom of the foundation wall to the top usually spells trouble so call in the experts get a proper evaluation and then feel comfortable with the pricing and the task on hand before moving forward with a house with Foundation repairs.

9.Another very important one is your HVAC Contractor-Always make sure you're heating and cooling systems are working properly and up to date. There is nothing better for a buyer then walking into a home and scoring a brand-new heating and cooling system. The feel of clean warm air coming out of air ducts is nearly priceless. New vent covers, new thermostat, new shiny metal duck work and the best part a new furnace and AC Unit.

The comfort the buyer will have known that when its super-hot or super cold outside they will not have to worry. All the large items such as Roofing, windows, Siding, HVAC, electrical, and appliances come with warranties. These warranties will provide buyer reassurance every time.

A couple more experts to always have picked out and ready to go are

10. asphalt contractor

11. landscaping sod company

12. Structural engineer

13. Architect

14. fireplace company

15 A builder just in case your project takes a huge turn

16. A tree company for trees that will need to be cut down or branches that need to be trimmed. Make friends with these contractors because they will help your circle grow and provide you with the confidence and support you will need.

    Below is a table of the average costs of the most common home improvement projects according to 2023 reports and by statistics this day and age. Remember that these averages are only estimates and prices can vary because of locations, personal preference and materials and the extent of the renovation.
    Our first item is A Full bathroom remodel which typically includes moving fixtures, new floors, adding a shower or new Bathtub and towel bars vanity and mirror.
    Our Second item is a full Kitchen renovation which typically includes new counters, cabinets, and floors. These costs are also completely dependent on the size of the kitchen, the materials used for instance a granite countertop can run a pretty penny these days....
    Our third item is new flooring throughout the main floor in the house that may include tile in the bathrooms and everyone's New most common flooring choice of the good old waterproof laminate wooden toned click and lock floors.

Average cost of 1 bathroom remodel in 2023	Most homeowners spending around $6,250	$4,500 to $9,000
Average cost of a Full Kitchen remodel in 2023	Most homeowners spend around $22,000	$20,000 to $25,000
Average cost of a flooring installation in 2023	Most homeowners spend around $5,000	$2,500 to $7,500
Average price of a full window replacement in 2023	Most homeowners spend around $450.00 per window	$250.00 to $600.00 per window

Unfortunately, all the replacement prices keep going up due to higher pricing and inflation because contractors are needing to charge more and more to be able to work.

Chapter 5
Buying, Making or Breaking your Dreams.

Cash is the simplest for flipping. With Cash buying you do not have to go through their mortgage application process and approval process, and the offers become more attractive to sellers turning on some headlights for them you can also do quick closes 7 to 14 days instead of the normal bank process of 30 to 45 days. Also, you will not have to worry about interest payments for the property as the renovations are underway. But a lot of house flippers need financing, based on ongoing statistics over 50%

Securing a Loan is an important step in your endeavor, there are Banks and hard money lenders may be able to loan quicker and faster than a bank. Most lenders will not lend to first-time flippers/buyers since they lack the successful financial track record lenders look for. Lenders see first time flippers with no experience as a risk to the business. While not all hard money lenders are resistant to working with a first-time investor.

Once you figure out the amount you will need for the property, you should investigate the detailed costs of the projects. Many house flippers make mistakes in these parts.

An example, if neighborhood pricing is around $200,000, you purchase the property for $125,000, a $15,000 bathroom upgrade will soak up quite a bit of your profit. So, if you limit your bathroom remodel to $5,000 instead you could use those other funds for something else or potentially save it for profit or a price drop later if you must negotiate a bit with a potential buyer.

Always look at the lower side of the market when purchasing or looking at potential buys for a flip .List 5 other properties at the least to do comparable on and don't start with the higher ones you will just be fooling yourself about the deal and in the long run ,let your own self down by doing this .A accurate CMA is so important so don't find a agent that will pull comps just to get the sale . A true agent will try and talk you out of a bad deal because they will want not only the buy but the listing later. The better the listing from the beginning

the easier the sale for them later. Remember the key is long-term not overnight success, if you want to turn to the stock market for that, and this day and age all you do is lose money there! Real estate is an asset, and it is a long-term goal that requires hard work skill and success.

Some of the most common mistakes when House flipping

1. Not estimating your cost correctly and spending way out of the budget amount, take it personally but don't take it too personally find an even barrier of passion.
2. Not having the support and the right contractors and group of reference ahead of time lined up. It does not matter how smart or talented or strong you are without a group of professionals that got your back house flipping is not possible.
3. Not paying attention to the market and the current trends and analysis of the time you are purchasing, rehabbing and selling the property make sure you investigate the advance and the past for reference.

3. Not paying attention to the market and the current trends and analysis of the time you are purchasing, rehabbing and selling the property make sure you investigate the advance and the past for reference.

4. Not doing your due diligence on the property you are purchasing, inspections even if you are buying as is so important. Doing your research will help you avoid pitfalls down the road.

5. Not having a projection of numbers put into place ahead of time and a backup plan to fall back on in case things take a sour turn and you need to liquidate quickly.

6. Not having a amazing real estate agent, having an agent that's got your back is so crucial to the whole process, remember interview lots of agents, make sure you click, and don't forget when you are making the money off of flips make sure they are well taken care of. A happy agent will work wonders for your potential!

I will share One of my experiences in an older home I had purchased- it's unforgettable. I had just swooped up this beauty built in the early 1920s in a historic part of town. The pricing was incredible. It had been listed for $50,000 right next door to a railroad.

I remember the first time I saw it looking up at the home slowly pulling in. The feeling was strong and sudden, and I was almost in awe and then also sadness. How weird to feel sadness and feelings for a home that I just saw. What was even weirder was that I had driven by that street and that home about a thousand times and never even saw it before and now these feelings were being felt.

I felt sadness when I looked at it because it was just beautiful but was so untaken care of, it was sparkling but dull, it was falling apart like an old swing set. I couldn't believe all the overgrown bushes everywhere, the falling branches, the trash everywhere. I couldn't believe that in the middle of this town nobody saw this happening slowly... Well, my disbelief turned into Love.

We walked the entire property inside and out and I had written my long, long list. This was one of the longest lists I had ever written when walking on a property, this would be one of my first most expensive flips yet. The whole house was completely gutted down to the great big red oak lumber studs. I could see them each one probably ran 16ft and weighed so heavy. When I walked there was not even One creak or crack every single piece of exposed wood was sturdy and just sat in its perfect place. The listing said possible tear down are you kidding this house was sturdier than any house within 5 miles from here. This house had such warmth without even a single piece of carpet or heat in it.

On one far right corner of the living room sat an enormous old fireplace, I just imagined the memories that must have taken place around a cracking warm fire. On the other side a gorgeous set of Victorians like steps leading up to a second story which was just one large open space. I immediately pictured a window seat and 2 bedrooms that would fit perfectly. The first floor was just one large open floorplan, it needed lots and lots of TLC. There was this huge what looked like to be old dining room which led out to a small, tiny falling 1920 's kitchen. The sink looked more of like a vintage artifact than anything that would be used to wash in, it was pink. I don't think I had ever seen a pink kitchen sink before. I saved that piece for sure.

What I wasn't looking forward to was the basement, I had caught a glimpse of it from upstairs because one of the back rooms on the first floor didn't even have flooring. But I knew in mind that the basement is always one of those deal breakers and I didn't want it to be. In this house I was hoping that the basement was in 1 piece, that the walls were standing straight, that it was not made of old concrete blocks pieced together. I was hoping for a miracle. I took slow steps down each step was as thoe a slow-motion movie clip. As I came to the final steps, they took a turn and only had a piece of plywood to walk across. I saw it the huge cold space I had been waiting to see. It was cold and smelt cold but not wet. It was crisp and not humid. It was old smelling but not stinky. The walls were poured concrete, thick and sturdy just like the upstairs. They were tough and strong with old metal posts anchoring the house up. There were all kinds of writings on the walls in spray paint, words of love and caring, hearts with initials around them. I had gotten that miracle I was hoping for.

    There was a secret wine cellar towards the right side of the basement that looked as tho used to be an old coal room back in the early 1900's.

Nothing other than the walls and flooring and structural beams were salvageable in the basement but I didn't care, my hope was fresh and renewed. Now it was time to make sure this home was mine and I could move forward with my million plans that were running through my mind. Now was the time to make my move, but how was this going to fit my budget with all these extensive repairs. I would have to offer less than the asking price, I would have to offer a lot less and would it work, would I still be able to get it, it was a lot of what ifs in the next day. I took my chance, and did it I offered $30,000 for the property, twenty thousand less than they were asking. I had too, I had to fit it in my budget.

    I wanted the house so much I could see all the repairs being made, I was visualizing every single room being fixed and made new again. I had the colors picked out, the landscaping pictured everything was mine and done already in my mind before we even got a response back.

The next morning my agent called with the news they had accepted the offer, there was a $28,000 lien on the property and the offer would be enough for everyone to finally walk away and be happy. Yes, this couldn't have been better, now if only the rest of the project would turn out like this, I would be smooth sailing.

Well, the rest of the projects was not smooth sailing because in flipping houses it seldom is. There were so many bumps and pauses during the process. There were times I would walk into the house and cry and wonder should of I should knock it down. There were surprises every day.

There was a large old propane tank buried that needed to be removed which exposed a whole bunch of Broken water pipes. All the water piping from the house to the main street had to be replaced,400ft to be exact. There was an old water cistern that was used in the day to supply water to the house that needed to be removed. There was a buried inground pool that was used as an old bathhouse which had to be dug up.

Day after day, month after month we worked and pulled help from this way and that way. The city got involved, the water district got involved. It was one of my utmost difficult rewarding flips ever. This home had become my time, my work, my sweat, my sleep, my stress, my thoughts, my emotions. This home had gotten my love, my energy, my ideas, my happiness and my continuous caring and attention. It was like a little puppy that needs constant attention the first couple nights you bring it home. That was what this home became, I called it my Diamond house.

Seeing this Diamond house gave a complete shine to it. It had its brilliant rise back to life. When others were thinking of tearing it down to build something that would shake every time the train drove by. I was thinking about its memories and history. I was thinking about who would live here and who would enjoy it as much as it had been before it was let go, before it had ended up in the wrong hands.

Chapter 6
Lets flip this Diamond Conclusion

Flipping houses can be an extremely rewarding, lucrative way to create wealth for yourself when done correctly. But you will run into a lot of mistakes and problems along the way. Make sure to research different real estate markets and locate thriving neighborhoods. You want to locate properties and areas where profits are completely visible. A growing economy and a jump in population are all great signs. Always stick to a budget, try starting small if you're a beginner, smaller houses, smaller projects until you get the hang of things.

Always keep costs on the lower end and spend, splurge towards the end of the project when you know exactly how much you have left to spend and the places where you may need to add. The best places to add extra funds if the rest of your project is completed is the landscaping, outdoors, kitchen and perhaps a spa bath to really get the deal sold!

Some last conclusive tips for your real Estate flipping dreams and projects.

- Planning time is crucial so have a team ready to help and on speed dial.
- Figure out your budget and numbers ahead of time, not once, not twice but three times to be on the safe side. Figure out the mortgage rates, the interest, the taxes, the property insurance all in advance so you are not caught by surprise.
- Use mortgage tools and do your research with other agents and house flippers in the area.
- Install a great relationship with your contractors upfront, find out their costs, their project specs and line them up in advance that way when you are ready to roll so are they!

When picking a property there are so many different important things we need to consider before taking that giant step and purchasing it. Always purchase with good intentions from the beginning. Always bring happiness and positive energy with you to the property. Yes, there will be times when you feel like crying or just giving up but that is just part of the process of growing as a flipper, as an investor. Every house more that you gain in this experience is every step closer that you achieve your goals and dreams.

Example Budget for New Build 850 sq foot split level in median average suburb area

Lots / Land and purchase $125,000

permits,plans,copies	$13,000
holding costs pipe work/pull in	
survey work	$2500
Demo / Tree work	$21,000

Equipment Rental / Equipment Purchase

Dump and Hauling	$40,000
holding cost	$2000 monthly
Excavation house driveway	$4500
Foundation / drain waterproofing	$16,000
rock / fill lumber	$1500
Lumber and Trusses	$19500
crane time	$1000

Rough carpentry labor	$2500	
Locks, assesories	$1,000	
windows and doors	$2,000	includes and and all additionals for interior cabinetry, window or door framing
framing	$8,000	
Garage/Doors framing	$8,000	
utility trenching	completed	overhead electric, underground phone ect.
sewer tap and water	completed	msd
flatwork and driveway flat	$4,000	concrete

total paid : _____

siding	6000
gutters	2000
roofing	6000
dumpster/trash	

total paid: _____

plumbing-bath-kitchen	5500
HVAC	6500
Electrical Temp Elec.	7500
Insulation	2000
drywall/taping	7000
painting	3000
flooring	4000
appliances	2500
cabinets	4000

1 refrigerator 1 stove, 1 dishwasher, and hood

counter tops kitchen	1000
trim materials labor	2000
vanity/trim material	2000

Chapter 7
Keeping motivation while flipping houses

Each house will come with its own set of problems which you will learn from and correct. Never take the shortcut when flipping a home, the short way is not always the best and might end up costing you more in the long run. No matter what anybody tells you, you're always going to have something to do with outside contractors electrical or Plumbing or HVAC or asphalt or concrete .

You have to have steady income first of all coming in when you're flipping or if you're deciding to quit your full-time job have some cash saved on the side for expenses and living .During the process you will not have money coming in from the properties but going out super fast. Remember to gather your lists and expenses ahead of time and remember they will never be accurate, in house flipping there is no room for accuracy. Because you do not how much you are investing in Each property. It is very easy to start spending money on a whole even though you have a budget it is easy to go over your budget.

Do not ever let anybody tell you the flipping a house is easy, it is not easy or fast. The amount that you're going to have to go through and go over is enormous. Hills and bumps, curves and holes will become regular with this industry.

Remember your courage when you buy and every better reason you are doing this along the way, it's because you're deciding to do it for yourself, for your family and for your future. You are deciding to go over what you normally do, you are an overachiever, and this is your first step to overachieving.
This is your step to helping your life have more Freedom, more flexibility and financial prosperity!
Remember that you are not only just flipping a house but that you are flipping a home somewhere somebody will live in and make memories, raise a family and grow in, grow up in and grow old in.

One of the most important things you want to keep track of is your estimates and estimating.
These estimates on your jobs are so important to be able to work with your budgets and stay in your
Pricing that you wanted to complete your project in, in the first place.

Whenever you proceed the first step to get your project off to the right start is proper, fair and competitive numbers for all the steps in your project.
If you take your time here and start organized it will help you not just in this project but for years and projects to come.
Gathering competitive estimates is crucial for your Budget.
So, I repeat take your time and do this process with as much patience as you can even with all the excitement and urge to start as soon as possible you need to give yourself this time to gather the info you need which will help you dramatically.

Calculate cost per square foot based on your past rehab projects.
<u>Use this to estimate rehab costs by multiplying it with the property's square footage</u>
Consult Contractors, Local Rehabbers:
Network with contractors to get pricing insights.
Compare line-item bids and refine your estimates.

Let's go over all the possible projects you will need outside estimates for.

1.So, starting from the Hat of the home the Roof in other words you need to be very careful with this one because this is an estimate that can vary drastically between contractors,

The Roof replacement is a very big expense to your Rehab project and can also help a lot for your selling potential and Overall Curb appeal to the property.

There are not cheap ways to replace a Roof so do not let a contractor tell you there is.

With experience and knowledge, I can confidently tell you that the cheaper way to do it is not the better route for a Roof ever.

A. To Install a new Roof and have a correct estimate put together for you it has to include, Removal of the entire old Roofing material no matter how many layers it has, never Reroof the Roof which means adding another layer of shingles on top of the existing layer of Shingles or Roof. Adding to a previous existing layer will just weigh the Roof down and always it will just cover what is hiding underneath and also any damaged or rotten wood that could be hiding underneath.

So all Roofing materials absolutely need to be removed, this includes the Roof, the Roofing underlayment called felt, then any damaged plywood or deck boards need to be replaced.

B.   Any damaged chimney flashings, Roof caps and Roof vents need to be removed.

C.   All Roof pipes, valleys where the Roof meets the siding, and Chimneys need to have flashings installed on the to prevent water leakages as those are key culprits of water getting in.

D.   Remember to get at least a 15 lb felt underlayment installed underneath the shingled Roof, make sure you pay attention to this material and that it is installed some not so trusty contractors try to skip this step as a money savings as this layer goes up quickly and often homeowners or property owners do not know this step has to be installed.

Next you will need to focus on the body of the property the siding, fascia wrap, the soffits, the window wraps ect.

This estimate can vary drastically. For instance, if you include the accessories if you don't. What type of fascia will you want, will you be adding Soffit will the soffit be ventilated or not, also what type of siding there are so many different items to choose from when it comes to the body of the house so keep watch closely and always gather multiple bids.

TIP: The world has a lot of scammers out there and it does not just exist in the stock market, crypto Pumps and in the movies, scams also affect property owners that are not well educated, so please Gather your education, your knowledge and all your info if you want to be a successful property flipper.

Some tools to help your house flipping go a little easier:
1. Market Research Understand local real estate trends, property values, and demand.
2. Property Inspection Tools:
A reliable contractor or home inspector to assess the property's condition.

Tools for various reasons to help with your understanding of the property, moisture meters, thermal cameras, and structural analysis software.

3. Renovation and Repair Tools:

Basic tools (hammers, pry bars, staple pullers) for minor repairs.

Sanders for refinishing surfaces.

Paint sprayers, power tools, safety gear.

4. Smart Home Features:

Enhance property value with smart home technology

Budgeting and Finances Create a realistic budget for your project.

Use software and spreadsheets to track expenses, profits, and costs

5. Team Building and Management:

Assemble teams of contractors, electricians, plumbers, and other professionals Tools for various reasons to help with your understanding of the property, moisture meters, thermal cameras, and structural analysis software.

3. Renovation and Repair Tools:

Basic tools (hammers, pry bars, staple pullers) for minor repairs.

Sanders for refinishing surfaces.

Paint sprayers, power tools, safety gear.

4. Smart Home Features:

Enhance property value with smart home technology

Budgeting and Finances Create a realistic budget for your project.

Use software and spreadsheets to track expenses, profits, and costs

5. Team Building and Management:

Assemble teams of contractors, electricians, plumbers, and other professionals

Manage and keep track of their schedules and tasks.

Some estimating formulas you can use to help your project run a little smoother from the beginning also include
1. Categorization and Line Items:
2. Tour the property, noting down issues and room conditions.
3. Condense your list into categories (e.g., plumbing, electrical, flooring).
4. Estimate costs for each item based on material, labor, bids
5. Per Square Foot (SF) Estimate:
Calculate cost per square foot based on your past rehab projects.
Use this to estimate rehab costs by multiplying it with the property's square footage
Consult Contractors, Local Rehabbers:
Network with contractors to get pricing insights.
Compare line-item bids and refine your estimates.

It is so important to Understanding the Scope of Work that your projects consist of the best way to start to understand is by Conducting a room at a time assessment of the property take a writing pad or iPad or something to write on to take thousands of notes split it up each Room at a time to make it easier to focus on what each Room needs before going into the next Room .Pay attention to everything in the Room from the floors ,to the walls ,to the ceilings , the blinds ,the windows ,the lighting ,the switches ,the outlets and the closets try not to cut any corners on your Room assessments as these can add up to extra costs down the road .

Distinguish the difference between structural improvements and cosmetic improvements, understand what is needed structurally for safety, guidance on all structural aspects if you yourself are not a licensed contractor as those mistakes made structurally are costly and also can provoke unsafe living environments.

Pay extra attention to larger tasks such as electrical, plumbing, HVAC those will impact costs and will need plenty of time and inspections to get done correctly .Remember there is never room for error when you are working on a property that will be occupied ,if you do things correctly then you will be able to sleep at night with no worries .Evaluate the age , condition, life left to all of the major parts of the property the roof, foundation, windows, doors, kitchen, bathrooms, flooring, paint don't spend where you truly don't need to and definitely spend where you are told too based on the condition even if it is a little more costly and you were not expecting it .
It is super important to always Creating a Realistic Timeline Divide your project into phases

Demolition-structural work-finishing touches ect and so on we show a little more of how to in the charts section of this book.
Identify your steps, process and priorities for example electrical work before drywall installation Floors before doors, paint before flooring ect.
And always Choose experienced contractors over non experienced don't cheat yourself by try to save a Dollar!

CHAPTER 8

In the Chapter we will review the going rates for different remodels in 2024.

---

1. Kitchen Rehab: Small to average Kitchen:
Average :26k
range: between $14k and $40k
huge Kitchen Rehab:
Average: Approximately $63k.
Value increase for Resale around $56k:

2. Average Bathroom
cost: $10k
Range from $2k to $80k
Walk-In Shower Installation:
Ranges from $3,500 to
$15,000. Bathtub $2k to $10

All pricing varies based on factors like location, materials, specific project details Contractor availability, size and specs, building codes and outcome wanted for resale.

3. Roof Replacement:
average price per sq pricing Between $290 to $390 per square
Per sq means a 10ft x10ft =100 sq ft section of Roof
Interesting enough if you open a insurance claim the adjuster will base their hail calculations based on a 10x10 section of your Roof . If they cannot find at least 3 to 4 hail hits in this section the majority of the time they will not cover it for hail damage .

Other remodel costs that ae based on size, location, trend, material type include but not limited to
Siding replacement, deck replacement, flooring replacement, painting, drywall install repairs and replacement.

Some astonishing prices that we will run through really quick just to give you a better perspective of where your pricing on materials should be at now.

Before COVID-19

Pre-COVID lumber prices were Stable. A thousand board feet of lumber cost around
$550.00 These prices were STEADY until the pandemic hit.

During COVID-19

Highest lumber prices during the pandemic. Highest ON RECORD lumber they went
from $550.00 to Around $1500 a thousand board feet Adjustments were made due to labor shortages at sawmills and the demand for lumber
due to the labor market staying at home trying to tackle their own construction projects.
Plus, the skyrocketing rehab and real estate sales left prices at the highest rates ever.

After COVID-19 Lumber prices fell significantly after the pandemic. now, they are
around $365 for 1,000 board feet lower than pre-pandemic levels
building materials, windows and doors, remain high due to labor-intensive production
and labor shortages

The real estate market also took a few hit during the COVID-19 PANDEMIC

Prior to the pandemic, real estate markets were stable. Prices varied but all together, the
market was pretty steady.

Millennials were reaching the age that they were beginning to purchase, and this was
helping with demand

During COVID-19:

It initially caused a slowdown in the housing market, lockdowns, uncertainty and pricing
became unattainable knowing if workers would stay employed.

But then remote work became more common, more workers began buying homes and
they moved further away from cities and centers .

Rental, home prices skyrocketed during this time, lower income houses experiencing job
loss and turned to alternatives like moving back in with family.

After COVID-19:

Real estate prices skyrocket again between March 2020 and March 2021 double the
gains across the country and added strength in most economies.

To conclude, a lot of what was before, what is now and what will be all arrows and
aspects point to a definite and accurate conclusion.

During times of struggles and times of need, times of strife, times of confusion there
are lots of ups and downs.

We need to seek physical assets to help raise the economic future of the next
generations. We have, like I had written earlier, a task.

That task is to prevail, reform and continue to expand the Real estate market for the
good and benefit of all.

Before →

← After

BUILD A DIAMOND
HOUSE

FIXING
A
HOUSE
MAKES
A

CHA
NGE

BUILD A
HOME

the before
CREATES THE DREAM

BE THE CHANGE

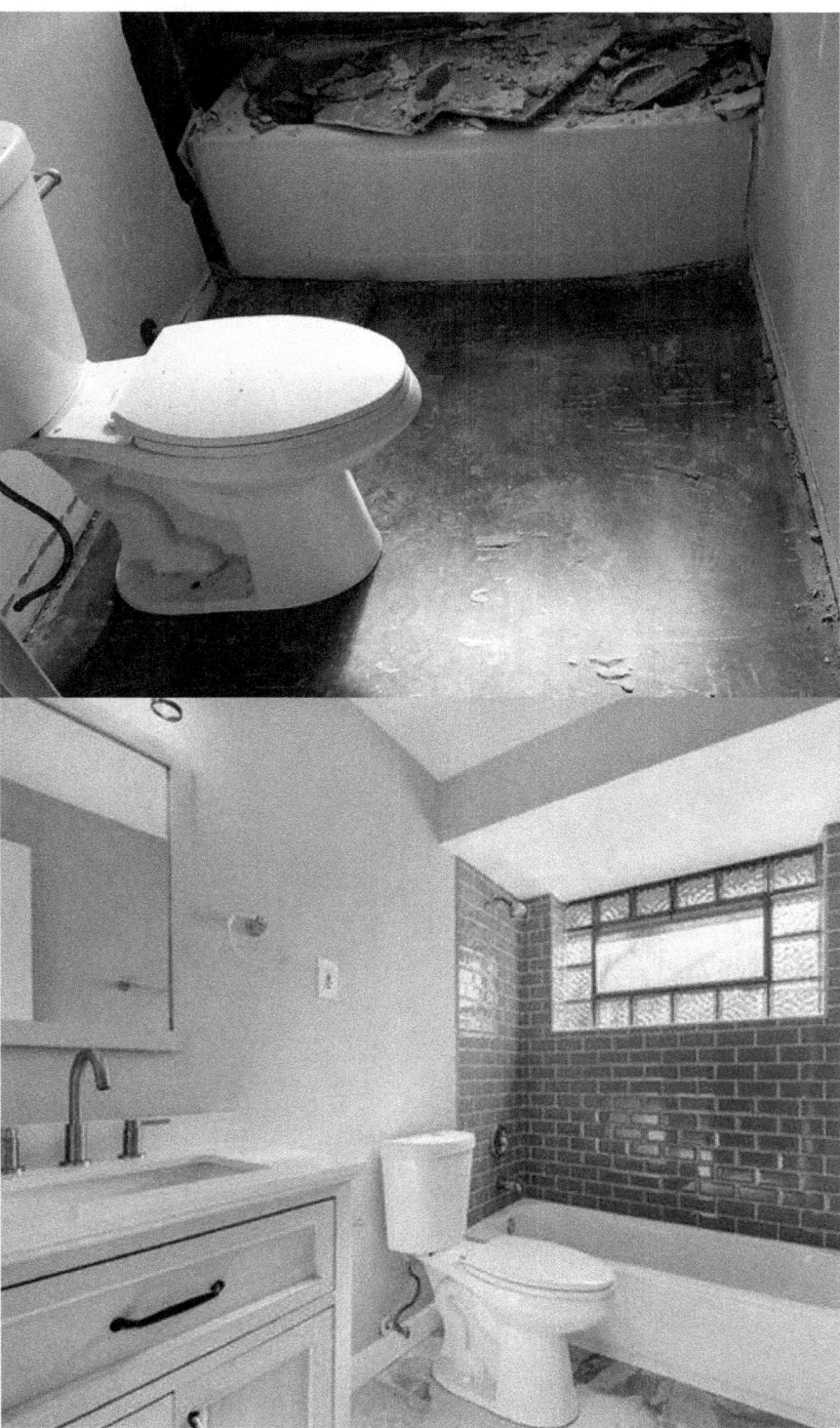

ALWAYS WEAR YOUR HARD HAT
SAFETY #1ST

work is work... machines do work ...

people control machines...

Before

driveways are the roads that lead you home

 **After**

THE BEFORE

THE AFTER

Sewer manholes going in on the site.

Be careful for large holes!
Watch Your Step!

THE MACHINES ARE IN THE HOUSE

to make a mess

DON'T FORGET YOUR
drain pipes

TO HELP STEER WATER AWAY
from your foundation

SOME OF MY FAVORITE FLIPS

COLOR OF SIDING MATTERS

THE START LEADS TO

A BEAUTIFUL FINISH

BEFORE

AFTER

Fresh driveway, careful don't leave your footprints!

BEFORE

MAKING THIS CALI-STYLE HOME MODERN AND SOPHISTICATED

AFTER

TAKE YOUR TIME AND BE PATIENT

TAKE PRECISE MESUREMENTS

THE START OF THE FRAMING

BUILD

BUILD

ORGANIZATION

MANAGEMENT

Digging those trenches

Prior to excavating

always mark your

electric and power lines

Incoming! Clearing space for are apartments to go up!

AFTER A

long work day

BEFORE

AFTER

BEFORE

AFTER

before

after

NEW TILES

FOR CLEAN LOOK

Little machine, big trenches!

Your Essentials For House Flipping

Success

FOCUSING ON COST EFFICENCY AND TASK ACCOMPLISHMENT

Before you start your journey
into your house flipping ....
make sure you always have a
set list of all you'll need

your first step to dreams

create a design board

A crucial first step in the direction towards building a house- is making sure your organized and cohesive and stay on task. a design board helps your ideas cone to life.

what is a design board

A Design Board is an aesthetic perspective
The Purpose of a design board helps designers, builders, creators and crafter's conceptualize the overall design aesthetic.
It lays the outline for a project.

This is the initial step:
-the foundation for any project-
-the crucial beginning-
-the grand plan-

what is the scheme?

choose the main things now....

what are the ideas?

all the details... even colors!

what is your concept?

FROM THE
AUTHOR

Being in the industry for over 20 years has brought lots of ups and downs ,the truth hits when you decide to succeed, and it causes quite a stir until you have the pot mixed up correctly. Throughout the years of first-hand upfront experiences, I have learned the real estate rehab flipping trade in all aspects and hope to be able to share some of those experiences and learning approaches to my readers. If through reading this book you are able to take with you even but one example or salt grain of knowledge that will help you apply and excel I am thrilled and have achieved a rewarding experience based on the time that was directed towards sharing it.

As house flippers /rehabbers, we need to continue to revitalize and fix the communities in our home. We have this gift to give to there and fix what is broken. There are different levels in every state of life ,there are different professions and different specialties. You have found yours, and now is your time to use it accordingly. This is your turn to shine through your work and sacrifices, your perseverance.

The ideas and creations we create today will directly affect our tomorrow's. The ideas and creations we create today will directly affect the lives around us . These ideas and creations become the foundation for our future and for humanity that is to come beyond our years on this earth ,we should use it to the benefit of society as a whole and to our Earth.

So in conclusion, plant those beautiful memories along with the green trees of the earth. Plant the lilies and Roses along with your dreams as curb appeal. Create your footprints out of love and caring, thoughtful hearts . May you fix and flip with honesty and dedication, accurately and accordingly to correct terms.
May You be blessed in all your endeavors!

BEST REGARDS
ECO CONSTRUCTION

Your Essential Checklist

KEEP ORGANIZED

A simple Checklist

floor
wall
paint
landscaping
roof
doors
windows
carpet
insulation
siding
fascia
heating
cooling
lighting
utilities
appliances
bathroom
tiles
mirrors
fixtures

- [ ] floor ○ _____
- [ ] wall ○ _____
- [ ] paint ○ _____
- [ ] landscaping ○ _____
- [ ] roof ○ _____
- [ ] doors ○ _____
- [ ] windows ○ _____
- [ ] carpet ○ _____
- [ ] insulation ○ _____
- [ ] siding ○ _____
- [ ] fascia ○ _____
- [ ] heating ○ _____
- [ ] cooling ○ _____
- [ ] lighting ○ _____
- [ ] utilities ○ _____
- [ ] appliances ○ _____
- [ ] bathroom ○ _____
- [ ] tiles ○ _____
- [ ] mirrors ○ _____
- [ ] fixtures ○ _____

- [ ] floor _____
- [ ] wall _____
- [ ] paint _____
- [ ] landscaping _____
- [ ] roof _____
- [ ] doors _____
- [ ] windows _____
- [ ] carpet _____
- [ ] insulation _____
- [ ] siding _____
- [ ] fascia _____
- [ ] heating _____
- [ ] cooling _____
- [ ] lighting _____
- [ ] utilities _____
- [ ] appliances _____
- [ ] bathroom _____
- [ ] tiles _____
- [ ] mirrors _____
- [ ] fixtures _____

☐	floor	○_____
☐	wall	○_____
☐	paint	○_____
☐	landscaping	○_____
☐	roof	○_____
☐	doors	○_____
☐	windows	○_____
☐	carpet	○_____
☐	insulation	○_____
☐	siding	○_____
☐	fascia	○_____
☐	heating	○_____
☐	cooling	○_____
☐	lighting	○_____
☐	utilities	○_____
☐	appliances	○_____
☐	bathroom	○_____
☐	tiles	○_____
☐	mirrors	○_____
☐	fixtures	○_____

- [ ] floor   ○_____
- [ ] wall   ○_____
- [ ] paint   ○_____
- [ ] landscaping   ○_____
- [ ] roof   ○_____
- [ ] doors   ○_____
- [ ] windows   ○_____
- [ ] carpet   ○_____
- [ ] insulation   ○_____
- [ ] siding   ○_____
- [ ] fascia   ○_____
- [ ] heating   ○_____
- [ ] cooling   ○_____
- [ ] lighting   ○_____
- [ ] utilities   ○_____
- [ ] appliances   ○_____
- [ ] bathroom   ○_____
- [ ] tiles   ○_____
- [ ] mirrors   ○_____
- [ ] fixtures   ○_____

- [ ] floor _____
- [ ] wall _____
- [ ] paint _____
- [ ] landscaping _____
- [ ] roof _____
- [ ] doors _____
- [ ] windows _____
- [ ] carpet _____
- [ ] insulation _____
- [ ] siding _____
- [ ] fascia _____
- [ ] heating _____
- [ ] cooling _____
- [ ] lighting _____
- [ ] utilities _____
- [ ] appliances _____
- [ ] bathroom _____
- [ ] tiles _____
- [ ] mirrors _____
- [ ] fixtures _____

☐	floor	○_____
☐	wall	○_____
☐	paint	○_____
☐	landscaping	○_____
☐	roof	○_____
☐	doors	○_____
☐	windows	○_____
☐	carpet	○_____
☐	insulation	○_____
☐	siding	○_____
☐	fascia	○_____
☐	heating	○_____
☐	cooling	○_____
☐	lighting	○_____
☐	utilities	○_____
☐	appliances	○_____
☐	bathroom	○_____
☐	tiles	○_____
☐	mirrors	○_____
☐	fixtures	○_____

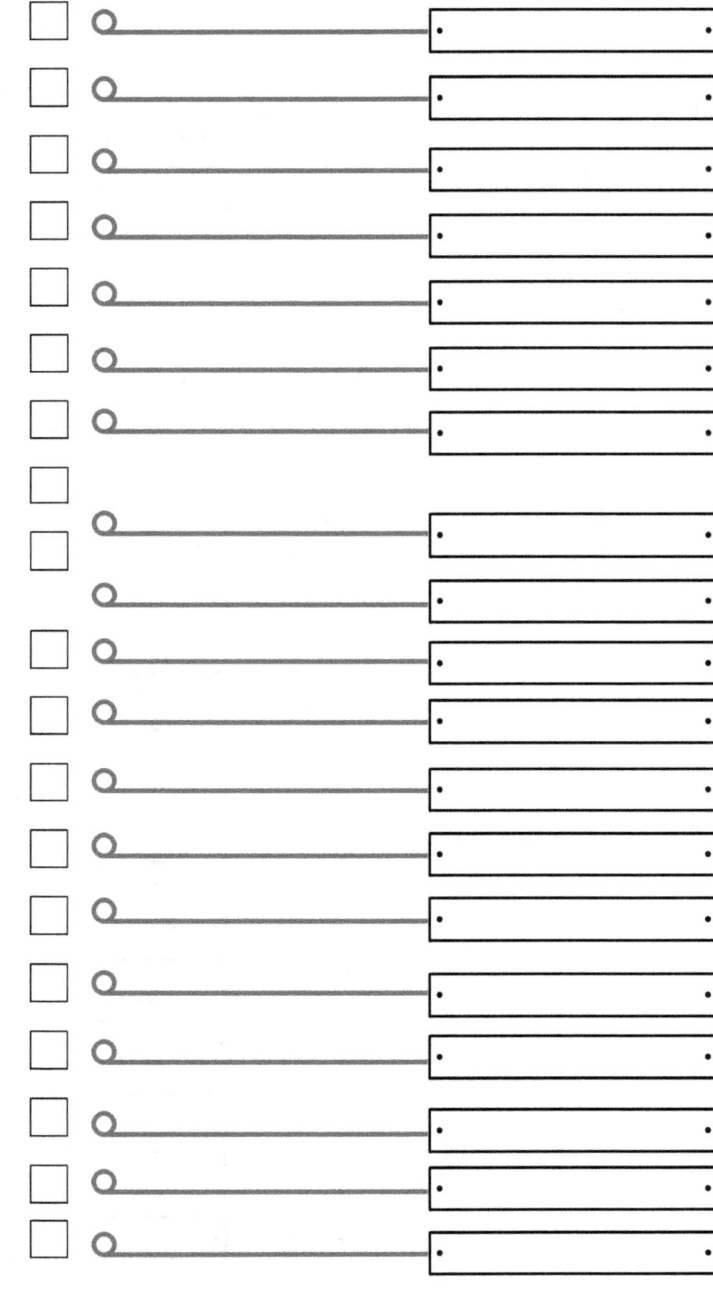

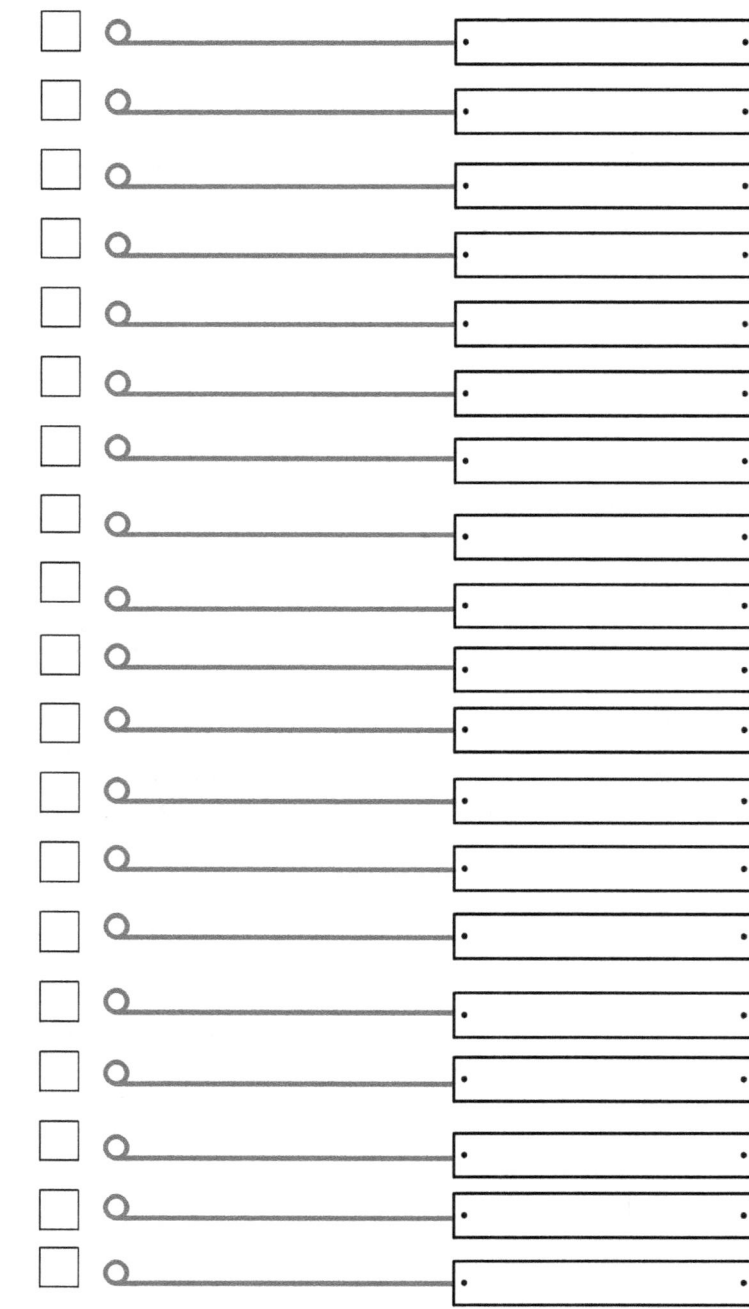

categories of project	estimated cost	net profit

categories of project	estimated cost	net profit

categories of project	estimated cost	net profit

categories of project	estimated cost	net profit

categories of project	estimated cost	net profit

categories of project	estimated cost	net profit

categories of project	estimated cost	net profit

categories of project	estimated cost	net profit

categories of project	estimated cost	net profit

categories of project	estimated cost	net profit

categories of project	estimated cost	net profit

categories of project	estimated cost	net profit

categories of project	estimated cost	net profit

categories of project	estimated cost	net profit

categories of project	estimated cost	net profit

categories of project	estimated cost	net profit

categories of project	estimated cost	net profit

categories of project	estimated cost	net profit

categories of project	estimated cost	net profit

categories of project	estimated cost	net profit

categories of project	estimated cost	net profit

categories of project	estimated cost	net profit

categories of project	estimated cost	net profit

categories of project	estimated cost	net profit

categories of project	estimated cost	net profit

categories of project	estimated cost	net profit

NOTES AND PLANS

NOTES AND PLANS

NOTES AND PLANS

NOTES AND PLANS

NOTES AND PLANS

NOTES AND PLANS

NOTES AND PLANS

www.ingramcontent.com/pod-product-compliance
Lightning Source LLC
Chambersburg PA
CBHW070454100426
42743CB00010B/1614